EVERYTHING TEEN GIRLS SHOULD KNOW!

101 Random but Important Skills That Prepare Teenage Girls for Life

Jenn Higgins

ISBN: 978-1-957590-35-6

For questions, email: Support@AwesomeReads.org

Please consider writing a review!

Just visit: AwesomeReads.org/review

FREE BONUS

SCAN TO GET OUR NEXT BOOK FOR FREE!

TABLE OF CONTENTS

SECTION TWO
ALL ABOUT YOUR BODY..21

SECTION THREE

ALL ABOUT GROWING UP **45**

SECTION FOUR
WHAT HAPPENS AT HOME...................................74

SECTION FIVE
WHAT HAPPENS ONLINE 102

SECTION ONE

ALL ABOUT YOU AND YOUR RELATIONSHIPS

Your experiences and your emotions work together to create the **core beliefs** you have about yourself. You can think of core beliefs as that tiny voice in your head that tells you things about yourself.

Sometimes this voice isn't very nice, so it's important to get to know your true self so you can learn to recognize when a core belief is damaging to you.

The most crucial relationship in your life is the one you have with yourself. It can seem silly to think about having a relationship with yourself in this way, but it will be impossible to pursue a healthy relationship with another person until you feel happy with yourself and comfortable in your own skin.

The best way to get comfortable with the woman you're becoming is to take some time to get to know yourself better. Explore what inspires you and consider how your core beliefs might influence your emotions, personality, likes and dislikes, and more.

[1]
INTROVERTS VS. EXTROVERTS

An introvert is someone who gains energy from being alone. Extroverts are energized by being around large groups of people.

To figure out if you're more of an introvert or extrovert, answer the following questions:

- Would you rather stay in and watch a movie tonight or go to a party?
- Do you prefer to work on school projects alone or in a group?
- Would you rather write a paper or give a speech?

If you prefer to work in a group or give a speech, you're probably an extrovert. Extroverts thrive with others and may feel tired and sad when they aren't around people for a long time.

You're likely more introverted if you picked watching a movie or writing a paper. This doesn't mean you don't enjoy parties, but introverts like to be alone to recharge their batteries after being around other people.

While no one fits perfectly into one type over the other, knowing what inspires and excites you can help you make friends, succeed in school, and boost your self-confidence.

[2]
COMMUNICATING
YOUR EMOTIONS

Knowing what energizes you can provide insight into what makes you happy, sad, or angry. But what about those other, more complicated emotions? Like when you feel a mix of sadness and anger at the same time? Or when you feel so happy, you could just cry?

Your emotions have many layers, so talk about them one at a time to understand how each influences the other. Many emotions are connected to one another. Something that might help are reviewing emotion charts online. Although there are many forms of these online, most of them are represented in the form of a wheel and illustrate how emotions are related.

For example, feeling both surprise and sadness can lead to feelings of disapproval, while feelings of sadness and disgust can lead to remorse. These are both sad emotions, but they feel very different. Here are some words you can use to communicate how you feel:

[3]
HOW TO CALM
YOURSELF DOWN

Sometimes emotions can be overwhelming—we can laugh ourselves silly or meltdown into a tantrum. Stress and anxiety can also make it hard to fall asleep at night or pay attention during the day.

When you're feeling very strong emotions and need to calm down, ask to be alone until you feel better. Once you're alone, it can help to write in a journal or try these self-soothing techniques to calm yourself down:

- **Practice square breathing.** Breathe in deep for four seconds. Hold that breath for four seconds, and exhale for another four seconds. Relax and count to four, then start over again.

- **Give yourself a hug.** Take a deep breath and exhale as you wrap your arms around yourself. Give yourself a little squeeze and say, "I've got this."

- **Hypnotize yourself.** You can trick your mind into relaxing with soothing phrases. Try sitting in a chair and repeating to yourself, "My right arm is heavy. My left arm is heavy. I am heavy and calm." Take a deep breath and repeat this four times.

[4]
HOW TO MEDITATE

Meditation is a mindfulness practice that uses the square breathing technique. Before you start, find a comfortable seat on your bed, at your school desk, or on the floor. Next, set a timer. You want to meditate for at least five minutes, but you can set it for anywhere from five to twenty minutes.

To start, close your eyes and take a deep breath. Count to four, then exhale and count to four again. Relax for four seconds, then repeat. Keep your eyes closed and pay attention to how your breath sounds as it goes in and out of your nose. Does it whistle? Is it silent?

Let your mind wander through your body. Notice how it feels in your feet, at your knees, and even on the top of your head. Keep breathing and counting to four. If you start daydreaming, just think about how your breath feels in your nose and start counting again.

When the timer goes off, take a deep breath and open your eyes.

[5]

HANDLING DISAPPOINTMENT

Disappointment happens when things don't work out the way you want. For example, you may have studied really hard for that history test and still got a D, or maybe you lost your last soccer game after a winning streak.

Disappointment can make you feel sad or angry. Some of the calming exercises above can help you handle disappointment in the moment, but you can also try:

- **Keeping things in perspective.** Disappointment can seem SO BIG when it happens, so give yourself time to think about the situation. For example, one bad game doesn't mean you're a terrible soccer player.
- **Looking for solutions.** Find ways to avoid repeating the same disappointments. For example, after failing a test, try asking a friend or your teacher for help before the next one.
- **Distracting yourself.** Distract yourself with an activity you're really good at to remind yourself how great you are, even when you make mistakes.

Unfortunately, failure and disappointment are a part of growing up. It's important to acknowledge how you feel and work through the emotions, but don't let disappointment dominate your whole day.

[6]
KEEP MOVING FORWARD

Everyone makes mistakes and fails every once in a while. Just remind yourself to keep moving forward. Don't let one mistake hold you back from trying again. After all, the word "fail" stands for "**F**irst **A**ttempt **I**n **L**earning."

You can't expect to know everything on your first try. The truth is, if you succeeded at everything, you wouldn't know how to do anything very well. Mistakes are how you learn.

Every time you make a mistake, you have to think of a new way to do it, making your brain work overtime to find a solution. However, trying the same thing over and over again is frustrating. It can make you want to give up — don't!

Instead, take time to celebrate your mistakes by walking away from the task and thinking about what you did right. Ask yourself, "What did I learn from this situation?" and "How will I do it differently next time?"

Failure isn't easy, so don't forget to congratulate yourself on handling a stressful situation. When you move forward with a positive attitude, you can think about failure without feeling embarrassed, angry, or sad.

[7]
ASKING FOR HELP

Asking someone for help after making a mistake isn't easy. You might feel embarrassed or frustrated, and talking to another person is the last thing you want to do. But even adults have to ask for help sometimes.

Empower yourself to ask others for help by practicing the following statements:

- "Here's what I was thinking. Do you have any suggestions?"
- "I've tried ____ and ____. Now, I don't know what to do. Can you please help me?"
- "I understand this part, but I'm confused about ____. Could you please explain it to me?"

Asking questions is part of asking for help, so if you're confused about something in school or something that your friends are talking about, speak up and ask for an explanation. It's likely that someone else is confused, too.

[8]
SPONTANEITY

Spontaneous people are more likely to step out of their comfort zones and try new things. Growing up will introduce you to all kinds of brand-new experiences, and the more you practice being spontaneous, the more confident you will be in these unfamiliar situations.

Try being spontaneous by breaking from your regular routine this week. Go big and sign up for a new after-school activity, or start small by watching a new TV series or movie that's completely different from your favorite genre.

Spontaneity doesn't have to happen all at once, either. Take it slow by looking critically at your daily routine and writing down the worries that are stopping you from doing things differently. Once you see what's holding you back, you can start to plan ways to add spontaneity into your routine.

Try picking out a new study spot at the library or walking a new way home. The trick here is to promise yourself you'll say yes to any new opportunity that comes your way, as long as it's not illegal or harmful to anyone or yourself.

[9]
MAKING FRIENDS

Your friends will influence many of your decisions as you grow up, so it's important to surround yourself with positive people who support you. Ask yourself the following questions about your friendships:

- Do you like having a lot of friends or just one or two close friends?
- Do you have a best friend?
- Is there someone new you'd like to be friends with but don't know how to start that conversation?

Good friends may not always share the same interests as you, but they will respect your differences and accept you for the person you are.

You might already have a best friend, but soon you will be heading into middle and high school, where you will sign up for sports, clubs, and new activities, providing the opportunity to meet all sorts of people your age.

One of the easiest ways to make new friends is to be approachable. Greet people with a smile and maintain eye contact when you introduce yourself. Using positive body language like this encourages people to feel comfortable around you.

Once you introduce yourself, you can practice striking up a conversation with some of these questions to get to know someone:

- What would you do if you were famous?
- Where did you last go on vacation?
- What's your favorite movie?

Start talking about some of the things you like and look for people with similar interests. You'll find that conversations come more naturally with certain people, and you might feel really good hanging out with them more than others. Pay attention to these feelings because these people are most likely to become your friends.

[10]
MISSING YOUR FRIENDS

Life takes us in many different directions, and sometimes you will have to be away from the people you like the most. However, as long as you reach out and talk regularly, no amount of distance will change your friendship.

Luckily, there are many ways to reach out to your friends when you can't see them every day. Start by sending them voice chats or text messages. Writing letters is another excellent way to keep up with friends you don't see very often.

A creative way to stay in touch over long distance is to create a letter journal. Take a plain, lined notebook, decorate it with your favorite things, and write your friend a letter inside. Then, mail it to them and ask them to respond with another letter in the notebook.

[11]
HOW TO BE
A GOOD FRIEND

Learning how to be a good friend starts with three L's:

- Listening
- Laughing
- Loyalty

Listen to your friends when they talk and let them have your full attention. Hear what they have to say and respond by asking questions or offering comfort if they need it.

Laugh with your friends. Friends are there to build each other up, and you can rely on one another for a smile or a laugh on a bad day.

Loyalty is the trust your friends have that you will support them. Loyal friends are honest with one another, apologize when wrong, and won't ask you to do things you don't want to do.

[12]
HOW TO RECOGNIZE A GOOD FRIEND

Different types of friendships exist, and people have many different ways of expressing love and affection. Not everybody will be a good friend in every situation. For example, one friend might make you laugh but not be very good at keeping secrets.

Recognizing how people treat you is important in figuring out if they're a good friend. The most common ways people express friendship are:

- **Words:** Good friends will communicate how they feel. They may pass you notes in class, send you text messages, or be comfortable sharing secrets with you.
- **Gifts:** Some friends express love by giving gifts, but these gifts can come in many forms. A good friend could save you a seat on the bus or at the lunch table, or they may bring you a new pen or let you borrow their clothes.
- **Time:** Good friends will want to spend time with you. The best time spent with friends can be when you do nothing together but talk and laugh.
- **Touch:** Some friends express love with hugs, fist bumps, or a secret handshake.

Which love language is most common among your friends?

[13]
UNDERSTANDING OTHER PEOPLE'S PERSPECTIVES

Aren't friends supposed to agree on everything? What happens when you disagree? Taking on their perspective can help you understand where your friend is coming from and could lead to an agreement.

What is perspective? Perspective is how you see things from where you're standing. For example, if you were facing your best friend and drew a capital "M" on a piece of paper, your friend would see a "W" — but you two aren't going to argue about that because you know it looks like a "W" from where they stand.

This is called perspective-taking. It means considering how different life experiences might influence how other people think.

When you meet someone new at school or while out with your friends, they might have a different opinion than you. The best way to take on someone's point of view is to ask them about it. Talking it out is the most straightforward way to understand someone else's perspective and learn something new.

[14]
HOW TO APOLOGIZE

Perspective-taking is also an important part of learning how to apologize. Giving a sincere apology involves understanding how you hurt someone and empathizing with their feelings.

If you need to apologize to someone and aren't sure how, follow these five steps to give a sincere apology:

1. **Say what you did wrong:** "I'm sorry for ____. What I did was wrong."
2. **Empathize:** "I know what I did hurt you/upset you/worried you."
3. **Explain how you will fix the situation:** "Next time, I will _____ instead."
4. **Ask for forgiveness:** "What can I do to make you feel better?"
5. **Let it go:** "Thank you for listening to me."

Always ask for permission before you start to apologize. The other person may not be ready to see or speak with you, and you should respect their boundaries. If you cannot apologize to this person face-to-face, you can write them a letter or send them an email or message on social media that they can read whenever they are ready.

[15]

HANDLING BULLIES

Just because you made a mistake and are apologizing doesn't make you a bully. Still, it's important to recognize when your behaviors harm others—and when someone else's behavior is harmful to you.

Bullying can take many forms, from verbal insults, teasing, and physical aggression to more subtle actions like talking about someone behind their back, spreading rumors, or excluding a person from a group.

If you're being bullied at school, it's important to tell an adult. Unfortunately, some bullies just don't quit, even when teachers and parents intervene. If this happens to you, you can try the following tricks to handle bullies at school:

- **Use the buddy system.** Walking with a friend to class or eating with a group of friends at lunch can deter a bully from picking on you.
- **Protect your feelings.** Bullies almost always want a reaction. They might leave you alone if you can ignore them or keep yourself from responding angrily.
- **Stand up for yourself.** No one has the right to be bullied. Stand up for yourself by telling your bully, "I don't care what you think," or "Stop bothering me."

[16]
STANDING UP
FOR YOURSELF

Acting bravely and standing up for yourself is hard. Feeling insecure can make you want to crawl underground and disappear. But no one has the right to make you feel intimidated or uncomfortable.

Building your self-confidence can give you the courage to stand up for yourself and talk to other people about how their behavior is affecting you. Knowing what you want to say ahead of time will make you feel less nervous when you approach them face-to-face.

Be assertive and kind once you know what you want to say. Practice with some of these assertive statements:

- "I don't like when you tease me about ____. Please don't do it anymore."
- "Can we talk about something else? I don't like when you make fun of me."
- "It would mean a lot to me if you would ____."

Practice what you want to say in front of the mirror. Writing it down first might help you organize your thoughts and feelings, too.

[17]

SETTING BOUNDARIES AND SAYING NO

Setting boundaries and saying no is an important part of standing up for yourself. The people you meet as you grow up may do things, or ask you to do something, that you aren't comfortable with — and you have the right to say "no."

What is a boundary? A boundary is an invisible line between you and the world, protecting you from anything that makes you uncomfortable.

What does it look like when someone crosses your boundaries? That depends on how you feel.

For example, you could be talking with a friend, but the conversation turns to a topic you don't like. Someone may also cross your boundaries if they start hitting, bullying, or bossing you around.

If you need to set boundaries with someone, try saying "no" in different ways:

- "Please stop. I don't like this."
- "No, thank you. I don't want to do that right now."
- "We played your way for a while. Let's play this way now."

A friend will never keep asking you to do something you don't want to do. If someone doesn't take no for an answer, find an adult you trust and tell them what happened.

[18]
BEING HAPPY WHILE ALONE

When you feel lonely, you can reach out to a best friend or parent, but you can also turn to someone else—you! You are a wonderful person, and you should spend your alone time getting to know yourself better.

Next time you're alone, try daydreaming about the things you like most about yourself and who you might want to be in the future. This might help uncover some fun activities you can do on your own that make you feel good about who you are, such as writing, coding, sewing, painting, or birdwatching.

You can also use your alone time to pamper yourself and work on your self-confidence. Give yourself a manicure or soak in the bathtub with your favorite book to really indulge in how wonderful you are. And don't forget to shower yourself with compliments!

[19]

WHAT TO DO WHEN
YOU LIKE SOMEONE

As you get to know the new people around you, you might find that you like a certain someone more than the rest. What does it mean when you like someone as more than a friend? This is called having a crush, and it means you should get to know them better.

When you like someone, learn as much about them as you can. Ask them questions about their hobbies and family. Showing interest in their life is a great way to engage them in conversation and discover whether you genuinely like them as a person. You may find that you have a lot of things in common.

What if you're too nervous to talk to them? The best part about having a crush is that they never have to know. There is no rule saying you have to ask your crush out on a date or even speak to them.

Try embracing these new feelings about your crush by creating a playlist of the songs that make you think of them. Sometimes it can be fun just to enjoy the secret or share your excitement with your closest friends.

SECTION TWO

ALL ABOUT YOUR BODY

Right now, your body is going through some pretty big changes that may require you to pay extra attention to yourself. Pimples and periods, tampons and bras—it can be a lot! So, remember to always be kind to yourself, even when you're feeling frustrated and confused about what's happening as your body changes.

When you'll start puberty depends largely on genetics. Some girls start their periods as young as eight years old, while others won't experience puberty until sixteen or older. If you are what some people refer to as a "late bloomer," it is a good idea not to panic and simply express any concerns you have with your doctor.

It's important not to compare yourself to other girls—not even your mom or your sister! There isn't just one right way to experience puberty, and your timeline will be unique to your own body. Your only job is to listen to your body and take care of yourself. That means understanding what's happening inside your brain and how it changes your skin, hair, and intimate areas.

[20]

YOUR BRAIN CHANGES DURING PUBERTY

Most of the changes that happen during puberty you won't even see. Inside, your brain is going through a metamorphosis that will impact how you think and feel. This is completely normal.

During puberty, your hormones start to change. Hormones are the chemicals at work inside your brain and body, guiding your physical and emotional development. Estrogen and testosterone are the two hormones responsible for most of your brain changes, but the side effects can give you mood swings.

You might feel great one moment and suddenly angry the next—let it out! Your emotions can disappear as quickly as they flare up, so let yourself experience these changes, and then let them go.

No matter how you're feeling, don't lock your emotions inside. Talk about your emotions with someone you trust. Your best friends may be going through the same changes, and it can help to share your moody thoughts with each other.

[21]
LISTENING TO
YOUR BODY

Mood swings are normal during puberty. Giving yourself space to feel these emotions is important, but it's also important to learn how to help yourself feel better.

Listening to your body takes practice and a lot of trial and error until you figure out exactly what your body needs. Take time to sit with yourself in silence and think through your day to pinpoint what your body might need — you may have lost sleep, skipped a meal, or completely forgotten to drink water all day.

For example, weird cravings can crop up during your period, or a headache could put you in a bad mood and ruin an afternoon with friends. You could take Tylenol to get rid of the headache, but try and remember — when was the last time you ate? Could you be hungry or dehydrated?

As your body grows, it will require more fuel. You may eat more than you did a few months ago (especially during your period). Staying full can reduce headaches and mood swings, and something as easy as drinking water can re-energize you during a slump.

[22]

HOW YOUR BODY CHANGES DURING PUBERTY

Testosterone and estrogen will be working overtime in your body to grow new cells, which also means developing breasts and growing hair in new places. The best way to get more comfortable with these new physical changes is to get to know yourself better.

It may feel silly, but try standing naked in front of the mirror and saying hello! Do you notice anything different?

You might see some pimples on your skin or hair growing under your arms and on your genitals. Your breasts may be starting to grow, but there's no way to know how quickly they'll grow or how big they'll get. They may even be different sizes right now, but they'll even out as you finish puberty.

You may also notice some spotting from your vagina around the same time your breasts begin to grow. Some girls will start their periods around the age of twelve, but yours may start earlier or later.

When your period officially starts, it will typically last for five to seven days. You will experience bleeding and might have cramps that feel similar to a stomachache. You have many different options of feminine products to use during your period to help you feel more at ease. The most popular kinds are tampons and pads.

[23]
HOW TO USE A TAMPON

Using a tampon for the first time can be intimidating. So before you start, take a mirror and look at your genitals. Use your fingers to separate your labia (the lips around your vagina), and you'll notice three holes: your urethra, vagina, and anus (or butthole).

Your vagina is unique to your womanhood — this is where babies emerge. While you're on your period, this is where you'll bleed. When you use a tampon, it will go inside your vagina and expand to collect blood and protect your clothing.

The tampon you use may have an applicator, a cardboard or plastic tube that holds the tampon. Without the applicator, the tampon will look like a cotton cylinder on a string. You will use this string to pull the tampon out of you.

To insert a tampon, sit on the toilet with your legs apart, or stand with one leg up on the toilet. Hold the tampon applicator with your thumb and middle finger, and keep your pointer finger at the bottom of the tube. Make sure the tampon's string is facing away from you, and insert the tip of the applicator into your vagina. Push gently on the bottom tube to insert the tampon.

If you choose not to use an applicator, wash your hands and unwrap the tampon. Hold it between your thumb and forefinger with the string facing the floor. Use your forefinger to feel your vagina, and gently slide the tampon inside. You won't have to change your tampon again for two to six hours.

You should not be able to feel the tampon once it's inside you. If you do, it may not be deep enough. If it's uncomfortable, take it out and try again.

[24]
HOW TO USE ALTERNATE FEMININE PRODUCTS

Unlike tampons, pads stay outside your body and stick to your underwear to collect blood. They come in different sizes:

- **Pantyliners:** for the beginning or end of your cycle.
- **Regular:** for the normal days of your cycle.
- **Heavy-duty:** for the heaviest days of your cycle.
- **Extra-long:** for wearing at night to protect your clothing and bedsheets.

To use a pad, open and unfold it from the packaging. When you unwrap it, you'll notice that the side attached to the plastic is sticky. Attach the sticky side to your underwear.

Some pads come with wings that unfold and stick to the bottom of your underwear to hold it more securely. Reusable pads come with snaps or bands that wrap around your underwear. No matter what type you use, it's best to change your pad every two to four hours.

Some women prefer to use menstrual cups instead of tampons or pads because they find them to be more comfortable. Diva cups are pliable and inserted just like a tampon—hold the cup between your fingers, pinch it closed, and insert it into your vagina.

Once inside, the cup will expand to catch blood. When you change your diva cup, sit on the toilet so you can easily dump it out. Then, wash your hands and rinse the cup with warm water in the sink before putting it back in.

[25]
SHOPPING FOR BRAS AND UNDERWEAR

Bra sizes are broken down into a number and letter—the letter represents the size of your breasts, and the number refers to the circumference size of your chest in inches.

Most bra sizes are between 28-44 inches, so measure your chest to find out what size you need. Take a tape measure and wrap it around your ribs, under your breasts, to get your chest size.

Average breast sizes are between AAA-DDD. You likely wear an A or B cup initially, so try on both in your chest size. You want to wear a comfortable bra that fully covers and supports your breasts without pinching. If your bra is too tight, try loosening the straps or pick a different size.

Underwear can be easier to shop for. It typically comes in sizes extra-small (XS) to extra-large (XL), but there are many different styles to choose from. Maybe you've already heard of some of them:

Like all clothing, bras and underwear are made for mass production. Different brands won't fit the same, so try different styles to find undergarments that fit your body comfortably.

[26]
CLEANING INTIMATE AREAS

Hygiene and puberty go hand-in-hand. The same hormones that make your breasts grow also cause acne and body odor. You will start to notice different odors, and you might sweat more than you did before, especially if you play sports.

Keeping yourself clean is the easiest way to reduce body odor and boost your confidence. But proper hygiene is more than just washing yourself with soap and water.

Starting your period will create new odors you've never smelled before. These scents are normal, and knowing how to clean this intimate part of you will keep you smelling and feeling fresh.

The vagina is a self-cleaning organ, and you don't need to use soap to keep it clean. You can use mild soap on the skin surrounding the area, including your inner thighs, but never put soap inside your vagina. This can cause irritation, so stick to warm water and a soft washcloth.

Wet the washcloth and use it to gently clean the areas under and around your labia, as well as your vulva and anus. Always clean from front to back when washing and wiping with toilet paper. This will keep bacteria from your anus away from your vagina.

Keep yourself clean by wearing comfortable underwear. Tight or ill-fitting underwear can make you sweat and irritate your skin, causing odor.

Never use feminine washes or deodorants in your vagina. If you're self-conscious about the scent, make an appointment with a gynecologist. Odds are no one else can smell it, but if something is wrong, your doctor will know what you can do.

[27]

CLEANING TOENAILS
AND FINGERNAILS

Your nails work a lot harder than you think, so clean your fingernails every time you wash your hands.

First, lather up and make sure the nails and tips of your fingers are covered with soap. Then, use your fingernails to clean under the nails on the opposite hand. Repeat with the other hand and rinse.

When you're in the shower or bath, you can give your fingernails and toenails the extra attention they deserve. Start with a washcloth and gently scrub your toes with soap and water. Use the cloth to reach under the nail and a nail brush to buff off any excess dirt.

Your nails will be the softest once you get out of the bath, so this is the best time to trim them. To cut your toenails, line the clippers up with the top of your toe, so the nail is the same length as the flesh. Then cut your nails straight across and use a file to soften any broken nails. Trimming your toenails and fingernails short keeps dirt from getting underneath them and reduces the likelihood of infection.

[28]
BRUSHING YOUR TEETH

Oral hygiene doesn't stop once you grow out of your baby teeth. The teeth you have now are meant to last all of your life, and the first step in good oral hygiene is finding the right toothbrush.

Use a small or medium-sized brush head that fits comfortably inside your mouth and around all of your teeth. Look for soft bristles that are gentle on your gums and enamel but tough enough to brush away plaque.

Next, pick out the right toothpaste. Stick with the flavor you like best but pay attention to how it feels when you use it. Does it burn your gums and tongue? You may want to try sensitive toothpaste.

To brush your teeth correctly, squeeze a pea-sized amount of toothpaste onto your brush. Start with your back molars and gently brush back and forth. Change to small, circular motions when you move to the front teeth to push the plaque away from your gums. Brush for two minutes, then gargle and rinse with warm water or mouthwash.

[29]

WASHING YOUR HAIR

The secret to washing your hair is not to do it every day. Shampooing every other day (every three days for thick hair) keeps your scalp healthy and protects your hair's natural moisture. Every woman has a different hair type, so it is important to conduct research and take tips from people with as similar of hair to yours as possible. For example, girls with straight, fine hair are more likely to run into issues with maintaining volume and keeping their hair from getting oily. Whereas girls with thicker or curly hair will battle with frizz, detangling and keeping their strands hydrated.

When washing your hair, use lukewarm water and comb shampoo through with your fingers. Resist the urge to pile it on your head with giant bubbles. This gets the product on your scalp, which can irritate your skin.

If you have curly hair or dye your hair often, you may need specialized products. For example, curly-haired products categorize patterns by a number and letter — types 1-4 refer to the curl families (from straight and wavy to spiral and coiled), and types A-C indicate how tight your curls are.

You can also try natural products, such as coconut oil and apple cider vinegar. Coconut oil is an excellent leave-in conditioner for curls—finger-comb it through your hair after the bath to lock in moisture.

If you have a dry scalp, dilute two tablespoons of apple cider vinegar in two cups of water and gently rub it evenly into your hair and scalp after shampooing. Let it sit for at least two minutes before rinsing.

When you shampoo and condition your hair, it is a good idea to do it facing down and comb your locks forward. This will help add volume to your hair while in the shower. Concentrate conditioning products on the ends of your hair. Oil is produced at your scalp, so the ends of your hair end up receiving the least amount of your natural oils to nourish them. This is also helpful in remembering whenever your hair is oily—you can use a boar's brush to distribute the oils from your scalp down the shaft of your hair. Past generations would do this by brushing their hair with one hundred strokes

[30]
TAKING CARE
OF YOUR SKIN

Acne is a common skin condition that can make you feel awkward and self-conscious. The good news is there are plenty of tried-and-true products to help you take care of your skin.

Stick to gentle cleansers that don't burn your face. Irritating your skin might feel like it's clearing up pimples, but it's actually making it worse!

The fastest way to get rid of zits is to wash your face every morning and night with a mild cleanser and lukewarm water. Spot treat pimples with a cream or cleanser with salicylic acid, which washes away the dirt and dead skin that clogs pores and causes breakouts.

Always moisturize with a lotion designed for your skin type. Oily skin still needs moisture, so focus on face lotions with ceramides. If you have dry skin, consider an ointment instead of a cream or lotion.

Finally, sunscreen is the most important part of taking care of your skin. Most face moisturizers come with an SPF of 10 or 15, which is all you need on an average day. However, if you plan on spending the whole day outside, apply a stronger SPF to your face, neck, arms, and anywhere else that will be exposed to the sun.

[31]
HOW TO SHAVE

Shaving is optional. Some women choose to shave their legs, armpits, and pubic hair. What you choose to shave and when is entirely up to you.

Start by familiarizing yourself with the different types of razors. Disposable razors are the most common, and you will have the option of choosing a three- or five-blade razor. Five blades are recommended as you're less likely to nick yourself, but three blades are better for sensitive skin.

To shave your legs, wet the skin and lather lightly with soap or shaving cream—never shave dry, as this will irritate your skin. Next, remove the safety cover from the razor and lightly press the blades against the skin above your ankle. Without ever lifting the razor, gently pull it up to your knee and back down again,

Continue this up-and-down motion around your shin, never lifting the razor. Once you finish with the front of your leg, rinse the blade and repeat the process on your calf. Rinse the blade again and repeat the process on your thighs. When you shave your knees, bend your leg and gently guide the blade up and over your kneecap to avoid cutting yourself.

To shave your armpits, lather your underarm in soap and raise your arm in the air. As you shave with your other arm, you will want to guide the blade downwards to reduce ingrown hairs and pimples.

[32]
DOING YOUR OWN LAUNDRY

Doing your own laundry is pretty easy once you figure out what all the buttons on the washer and dryer do. But first, start with sorting your clothes by color and piling similar fabrics together.

On the washer, choose your cycle:

- **Normal cycle** tumbles and spins fast and is the most common wash cycle for your clothes.
- **Permanent Press** tumbles fast but spins slowly to reduce wrinkles on dressier clothes.
- **Delicate cycles** are for hand-wash-only clothes, your bras and underwear, and any item of clothing you don't want ruined in the normal cycle wash.

Next, you want to wash your clothes on cool or warm/cool cycles. Hot water may sound nice, but it fades the color and can damage more delicate clothes. Save hot water for blankets and bedsheets.

Then, add your detergent.

If you're using a pod detergent, drop it into the wash with your clothes, close the lid, and hit start.

Dryers have normal and delicate cycles like washing machines, but other dryer cycles include:

- **Bulky** for bed sheets and blankets
- **Activewear** for delicate workout items made with synthetic fibers
- **Heavy duty** for thick fabrics that can take longer to dry, like winter coats or heavy blankets

If you're unsure how to wash or dry a particular item of clothing, read the back of the tag. It will give explicit directions on how to clean your garment.

[33]
SHOPPING FOR CLOTHES

Shopping for clothes can be nerve-racking when your body looks and feels different, but that doesn't mean there's something wrong with you.

The point of clothing is to fit well and make you feel beautiful, so follow these tips next time you go shopping:

- **Set a time limit.** You'll feel less overwhelmed by all the different options in-store if you know you only have an hour to find something.
- **Know what you're looking for.** Don't go shopping for clothes without an outfit in mind, or you'll be distracted.

- **Grab multiple sizes.** All clothes are cut differently depending on the designer, so find a piece you like and try on at least three different sizes.

Don't be discouraged when something doesn't fit you. Instead, focus on cuts and brands. For example, if you know boyfriend-cut jeans feel better to you than boot-cut, only shop at stores that sell boyfriend jeans. This way, you always know you'll find exactly what you're looking for.

[34]
WHAT TO DO WHEN YOUR CLOTHES DON'T FIT

As you grow, your weight will fluctuate. Along with your breasts, you might notice yourself getting bigger in other areas. Clothes that fit you a month ago may not fit you anymore, and it might seem like you should cut back on what you eat to fit into them again—don't.

It's important to eat when you're hungry and stop eating when you're full to maintain a healthy weight. Remember, if you still feel hungry thirty minutes after eating, have a little snack.

All of the changes you're going through require the vitamins and minerals you get from eating. Following a diet trend now can lead to malnutrition. If you need to go on a diet, your doctor will tell you and work with your family to create the right one for your growing body.

Instead, donate the clothes that don't fit you anymore, or host a clothing swap with your friends. Pick a weekend and tell your friends to bring all their old clothes. Throw them in a big pile, let everyone take their favorites, and donate the rest.

[35]
HOW TO DO YOGA

If you want to stay healthy and in tune with your body, try practicing yoga. Yoga positions for beginners can help you become comfortable with the poses.

Yoga poses help to stretch your spine and release tension in your muscles. And each one is low impact, making it the perfect workout first thing in the morning or right before you go to bed.

Some of the easiest yoga poses are:

Hold the child's pose and happy baby pose for five to ten minutes every day to help your body stretch and relax. When doing tree pose, alternate your leg lifts, and hold each side up for ten to fifteen seconds.

[36]
WHAT TO DO
WHEN YOU'RE SICK

To administer basic treatment, it's important to know how to describe and recognize different symptoms:

- **Fevers** happen when your body temperature rises above 100 degrees to fight infections and viruses. You will fluctuate between feeling hot and cold when you have a fever.
- **Body aches** happen when you feel sore all over but don't have an injury that causes you to feel pain.
- **Headaches** can be caused by stress, sickness, hunger, dehydration, or allergies.
- **Nausea** happens when your stomach aches and you feel like you might need to throw up.
- **Hives** are red, itchy bumps that crop up on your chest and neck, stomach, or behind your knees and are usually an allergic reaction.

If you're not feeling good, your symptoms are there to tell you what's wrong so you can do everything you can to heal your body and feel better.

For example, if you have a fever and body aches, you may have the flu. The flu is very contagious, so describe your symptoms to a parent or teacher and make sure you stay home from school. To fight the flu, rest and keep yourself hydrated.

Not every illness will have obvious symptoms. For example, you might have a slight headache one day and think nothing of it, but the next day your head hurts so badly that you can't open your eyes. A certain type of painful headache is called a migraine, and you may experience migraines more often as you progress through puberty.

The best thing to do when you're sick is rest. Stay in bed, watch your favorite movies, binge a new show, or close your eyes and listen to an audiobook. Avoid seeing other people for a few days until you feel better.

[37]
RECOGNIZING ALLERGIC REACTIONS

Certain foods, scents, or weather patterns can cause allergic reactions. Sometimes symptoms are barely noticeable, like a runny nose or itchy eyes. Other times they can make you feel sick to your stomach. Therefore, it's important to recognize how allergic reactions differ from the symptoms you feel when you're sick.

These are some mild allergy symptoms you might have when the seasons change:

- Itchy nose and eyes
- Sore or itchy throat
- Small, red rash (hives) or dry skin

You may also have more serious reactions to certain foods or weather patterns, including:

- Wheezing or shortness of breath
- Tightness in the chest and throat
- Vomiting or diarrhea
- Lightheadedness, dizziness, and headaches

When someone has a severe allergic reaction, they may go into anaphylactic shock. As a result, they may lose consciousness or stop breathing. Call 9-1-1 if this happens.

[38]
ADMINISTERING FIRST AID

How to administer first aid for minor injuries:

- **Cuts:** If you cut yourself, wash your hands and the wound with warm soap and water. Wrap the wound in a clean cloth and apply pressure to stop the bleeding, then apply a bandage. If the bleeding does not stop, see a doctor.
- **Burns:** Dull the pain by running the burn under cool water for one to two minutes. If the burn is severe, consult a doctor.

- **Blisters:** Popping blisters opens the wound to infection, so cover the blister with a bandage right away. Change the bandage every night before you go to sleep and again in the morning.
- **Nosebleeds:** Sit upright. Pinch your nostrils and tilt your head slightly forward to keep the blood from running down your throat. Maintain pinching for 10-15 minutes.
- **Bee stings:** Remove the stinger immediately and clean the wound with soap and warm water. If it's bleeding, you may need a Band-Aid, and the wound may bruise for a couple of days.

[39]
DEFENDING YOURSELF

Beyond the bullies you might face at school, learning to defend yourself can protect you in other situations as well. For example, a stranger may ask for help and then immediately grab your arms, hair, or backpack.

Try these six easy steps to defend yourself and get away to safety:

Step One: Scream as loud as you can.

Yelling "FIRE!" even when there isn't one will attract attention and encourage witnesses to call 9-1-1.

Step Two: Poke them in the eyes.

They can't hurt you if they can't see you, so hit them in the face and scratch or poke them in the eyes.

Step Three: Punch them in the throat.

Ball your hand into a fist and hit them in the neck as hard as you can.

Step Four: Kick them in the groin.

If you can't use your arms, kick them in the groin or stomach as hard as you can.

Step Five: Stomp on their foot.

This works best when someone grabs you from behind.

Step Six: Run.

Run away as soon as you are free and find a place to call the police as quickly as possible.

If someone attacks you, take advantage of your surroundings. Do you have a pencil in your pocket? Is there a rock nearby? Use anything you can to get away from your attacker.

Remember — not all nefarious characters hide in dark alleyways or break into your house when you're asleep. A friend or even someone you care about may try to hurt you. You can tell them to stop and defend yourself, even if it may hurt their feelings.

SECTION THREE

ALL ABOUT GROWING UP

Growing up comes with a whole new set of responsibilities. You'll notice that adults will start to hold you to a higher standard, and you may start to have some new expectations for yourself as well.

Just take it one step at a time. No one is in a hurry for you to grow up, and you have plenty of time to learn all of life's lessons coming your way.

"Adulting" may sound sort of silly to say, but this word incorporates all the actions you take on your way to adulthood. The life skills you learn now will impact the kind of person you become in the future.

While you're growing up, you have the chance to plan what your future life might be, and setting a goal is a great first step toward feeling like an adult. When you achieve that first goal, you'll feel a sense of confidence and pride in yourself, which is what adulting is all about.

[40]
SETTING GOALS

Goal setting is essential to growing up—it gives you a sense of direction. You'll always know where you're going in life when you set realistic goals to guide you.

The first step in goal setting is writing down something you want to achieve and the steps you'll need to take to complete that goal. Think about your strengths and what you like to do most.

How long will it take you to achieve your goal? Some goals can take all year to accomplish, while others may only take a few days, so give yourself a realistic timeline.

Prioritize your goals based on how long they will take and if any of them influence the others. For example, you can't play in a band if you've never played an instrument. So, start with a goal to practice an instrument every day for thirty minutes.

Always remember to give yourself time to celebrate each achievement along the way. If your goal is to finish the year with all A's, then be sure to give yourself a high five for every good test grade.

[41]
MAKING DIFFICULT DECISIONS

How do you know which goal to follow first? That's a hard decision you have to make on your own. You can ask friends, family members, and teachers for advice, but ultimately the choice will come down to you.

Follow these four steps to help you make a difficult decision:

1. First, identify the goal or the problem and how this decision will help you achieve or solve it.
2. Next, gather information about the issue. You can ask friends and parents for advice or research on the internet.
3. Then, consider the consequences—how will things change after you make this decision? Look at your decision from multiple perspectives to see what could go wrong or what might go right.
4. Finally, make your decision.

We can never know how our decisions turn out until we act on them. But you'll know you made a smart decision because you evaluated your goal, gathered information, and considered the consequences.

[42]

SCHEDULING APPOINTMENTS

Appointment-making phone calls should be polite and straight to the point, such as:

- "Hi, my name is _____, and I would like to schedule an appointment with Dr. ____."
- "Hello, I am a patient of Dr. _____. I'm calling to schedule an appointment."

The person on the other end may ask questions about your symptoms, your last visit, and what day of the week you want to schedule your appointment. Be prepared by gathering all the information you need before the call.

You might make other phone calls for appointments with teachers or academic advisors. Follow these scripts:

- "Hello, Mr./Ms. _____. This is _____. I'm calling to ask if you're free this week to meet with me to discuss the assignment."
- Hi, Mr/Ms. _____, it's me, _____. Are you free tomorrow to talk about my grade on the last math test?"

Sometimes, you can email or text to make an appointment. You want to remain polite, so open the message with "Hello, Mr./Ms./Dr. _____" and introduce yourself. The next line should state the reason for the appointment and how to reach you. Finally, close the message by thanking them for their time.

[43]
THROWING A PARTY

You will have plenty of opportunities to host all kinds of parties to celebrate the many milestones you'll reach as an adult. But hosting your first party can be kind of intimidating. Who will you invite? What will everyone do?

The first place to start is with friends. Who better to share this big moment than your favorite people? And once you know who's coming, you can plan a menu and activities around the things everyone loves.

One essential part of hosting a party is food. This doesn't mean you need to cook, but providing drinks and snacks is usually required if you invite people to a party. If you don't want to plan a meal, host a potluck and ask your guests to bring their favorite dish.

The next party element you'll need is a soundtrack. You can build your own playlist or ask a friend to put one together. The best part about planning a party is that friends will always want to help, so don't be afraid to delegate tasks to some of your guests.

Finally, you don't need to go overboard with party activities to have a good time. Sometimes a few snacks and a movie playing in the background are all you need. Consider the group you're inviting and plan three to four activities to bounce through to keep the energy high.

[44]
SPEAKING WITH CONFIDENCE

Speaking confidently doesn't mean talking louder than everyone else, but it does mean standing up for yourself and your opinions. As a young woman, it's important for your voice to be heard. You should never be made to feel ashamed to speak up.

But speaking up in front of strangers can be very intimidating! It's easier to talk confidently with friends because they make us feel comfortable, but sometimes we can feel embarrassed or too shy to speak up when we're around people we don't know very well.

Start talking more confidently by first taking a deep breath and then speaking slowly and clearly. Keep your tone friendly and casual, but stick to using "I" statements. For example, if someone is listening to music too loud for your liking, try saying, "It'd help me study better if it were quieter in here. Can you please wear headphones?"

Build your confidence by reciting lines in front of a mirror from your favorite movies or reading aloud from your favorite book. Pay attention to how your voice sounds, and try changing the speed and tone.

[45]
GIVING A SPEECH

Public speaking is often portrayed as one of the biggest fears among adults. Getting up in front of a room of people can be unnerving, even when you know how to speak with confidence. Just remember that the pit of nerves you feel in your stomach is normal—many people feel this way.

The easiest way to start your speech is to introduce yourself and explain why you're speaking about this topic. This can trick your brain into thinking you're just talking with friends and help keep you calm.

Give a speech with confidence by following these steps:

1. **Identify your topic and stick to the point.** Bring up the most important facts first, then include other information if you have time.
2. **Consider your motives and intentions.** Your intentions will guide your topic. For example, are you trying to convince the audience to take your side, or are you trying to make them laugh?

3. **Note your time limit.** Most school speeches are between two and six minutes. Knowing the length of your speech can help you better organize your topic.

Try using notecards to keep your speech on track. You can write keywords or phrases on the cards to remind you what to say, or you can write out the entire speech in case your mind goes blank when you walk out there.

[46]

HOW TO STAY ORGANIZED

Not everything you learn at school will come from a book. You will learn a lot by observing your own study habits and how you manage your time. You'll discover hidden talents and hobbies that can lead to fulfilling careers and relationships. You might even learn something new about yourself!

Staying organized is a three-tier operation:

- First, you have to organize your stuff.
- Second, you have to organize your study space.
- Finally, you have to organize your mind and avoid distractions.

To get started, gather your school supplies and organize them by subject or class period. Assigning a different color to each subject can help you remember when assignments are due and which folder or binder you're keeping them in.

You'll want to keep your pens, pencils, and highlighters nearby when you study, but you don't need expensive drawer organizers to keep your desk clean. Use mason jars or cut down old shoe boxes to separate your drawer space into sections and stay organized.

Finally, organizing your stuff and your study space will make it much easier to stay focused. Just make sure you have a special place to store your phone while you work so you aren't distracted. Whether preparing for a test or writing that final paper for history class, you'll want a clean, organized space that reminds your brain that you're there to study.

[47]
MANAGE YOUR TIME

Time management is one of the most important—and most difficult—adult skills to learn. Fortunately, getting organized makes it easier. When you know where everything is, you can start tackling your to-do list one task at a time.

Making a simple list can help you remember what you need to do, but it won't always help you manage your time. Instead, divide your tasks into four quadrants to help you prioritize what needs to get done first.

Steven Covey created a Four Quadrant System in his book *The Seven Habits of Highly Effective People*:

Divide a piece of paper in half horizontally and vertically so that there are four quadrants.

On the left side of the page, write "important" along the edge of the top square and "not important" along the edge of the bottom square.

At the top of the page, write "urgent" along the top of the first square and "not urgent" along the top of the second square.

You can divide these labels from the rest of the paper with a clean line to make it neater. Each square will represent a quadrant that you will fill with the tasks that need completing to help you determine their priority level.

Quadrant One is located in the top left square. These are the important tasks with an urgent deadline that you must tackle first, such as assignments due tomorrow and chores you need to finish today.

Quadrant Two is located in the top right square. These tasks are important but aren't waiting on a deadline, such as meeting with a friend about an upcoming group project or finishing a personal craft project.

Quadrant Three is located in the bottom left square. These tasks aren't important in the sense that you're earning a grade, but they're still important to you. Get to them quickly, but not before the tasks in Quadrant One.

Quadrant Four is located in the bottom right square. These tasks are for personal fun and enjoyment and have no deadline. Write in all the fun activities you have planned for the week in Quadrant Four. They might not have a deadline, but including what you're most excited about can make your hard work worth it.

[48]
IMPROVING
YOUR GRADES

Once you get organized and prioritize your tasks and assignments, you will see an improvement in your grades. You'll notice that it's easier to remember due dates and turn homework in on time when you keep your school supplies organized.

It can also help to organize your backpack the night before to make sure you have everything you need for the next day. Coming prepared to school each day is another easy way to improve your grades.

You can also use a weekly planner to stay on top of your assignments. For example, try using the Four Quadrant System in your planner to prioritize your homework, tests, after-school activities, and anything else you have to do by the end of the week.

If you have a busy week ahead of you, call a friend to do homework or study together. Studying with a partner can give you a new perspective on the subject and make it easier to ask for help about things you don't understand.

Never hesitate to ask questions and participate in class. If you don't understand something, the odds are that other students don't either. Most people are afraid to take part in class, but you can improve your grades by showing initiative, asking questions, and actively participating in your own learning.

[49]
GET A LIBRARY CARD

Library cards are completely free and give you access to books, computers, Wi-Fi, and other resources to improve your grades, research colleges, or play games online with your friends.

To sign up for a library card, head to the closest library and speak to someone at the counter. You must be a local resident to get a library card, so bring your ID and proof of address, like a report card or a utility bill addressed to your parents.

You will likely have to fill out a short application with your name and contact information. The library will use this information to contact you about overdue books or put you on waiting lists for new books.

You may have to wait a few moments while the librarian prints your new card. Once it's ready, sign it with your first and last name. If you lose your card, you may have to pay a small fee to replace it.

[50]
PICKING A HOBBY

What would you do if you had a free day to do whatever you wanted? The way that you answer that question could be a clue to your next favorite hobby.

Hobbies should make you feel good and give you a relaxing break from the stress of school, chores, and growing up. Consider these fun activities that could lead to several new hobbies:

- **Take a selfie.** Take pictures or film short videos with your friends. Play around with filters and stickers, or add a song in the background to see what you come up with.
- **Listen to music.** What's your favorite band? Put on their best album and listen to the different instruments. What do you hear? Anything you'd like to learn how to play?
- **Go for a walk or run.** Take advantage of the space around you. New hobbies are all around, and you may find one in gardening, soccer, or running when you get outside and explore.

- **Write in your journal.** Write down all the things you enjoy doing and why you like them. You may find that you like writing or doodling, which can lead to creative hobbies like painting, calligraphy, and storytelling.

[51]
VOLUNTEERING

Volunteer opportunities are available depending on your age and where you live. Most places accept volunteers who are at least thirteen, but some programs allow younger volunteers who come with their parents or family members.

To get started, research programs in your city that accept volunteers. Some of the most common places where teens can volunteer are:

- Food banks
- Animal shelters
- Libraries
- Habitat for Humanity

You can also find volunteer opportunities through your school. Programs such as Learn & Serve, Key Club, and Sierra Club specialize in community service and are an excellent way to volunteer with friends.

[52]
FILLING OUT
A JOB APPLICATION

You'll fill out most job applications online, but some places may still offer you a paper form. Either way, each job application will essentially ask you the same four things:

- Name
- Contact information
- Previous work experience
- Personal references

Personal references are adults who are not related to you but can vouch for your character. Good examples of references you can use for your job application are teachers, coaches, or neighbors.

If you don't have any previous work experience, don't panic. Everyone has to start somewhere, and many places are willing to hire someone who's starting their first job.

When you sit down to fill out a job application, read through the questions carefully. Think about what you want to say about yourself. Highlight your skills and list your experiences outside of the traditional workplace.

For example, write about the group project you coordinated with three other students or the game mod you coded. Employers will see that you have experience, and your unique skills will make you stand out from other applicants who are applying for the same job.

[53]
SETTING A BUDGET

Making a budget is easy — the hard part is sticking to it. So, try writing your budget in your journal or planner. Seeing it every day will remind you what you're saving for and keep you on track.

To start a budget, consider how much money you bring in from work or your allowance. This is called **income**. Compare your income to the necessities you're responsible for paying.

Are you responsible for a cell phone bill or car insurance? Budget for these things first and subtract them from your income. Then, compare the money you have left to the cost of the item you're saving to buy.

Before putting money away, consider the things you may need between now and your next payday. For example, you may want to set aside some money for school supplies or dinner with friends.

A good rule of thumb to remember is 50-30-20. This will remind you to spend half of your income on necessities, a third on fun things you do for yourself, and 20% should be put away in savings for that amazing thing you want to save up for and buy later.

[54]

OPENING
A BANK ACCOUNT

Most employers use what is called **direct deposit** and send your paycheck directly to your bank account on payday. A bank account gives you a safe place to keep your money, and you can use your bank's website or mobile app to keep track of your income and stay on budget.

To open a bank account, go into the bank and speak with a teller. Make sure you bring your I.D. Most banks will also require proof of address, just like the library.

You will need to make a deposit to officially open the bank account. Check with your bank to ensure you have enough to meet the minimum deposit — normally between $50 and $1,000.

Once you have an account, the bank will issue you a debit card that you can use to withdraw money from an ATM and pay for items at stores and restaurants. You will choose a unique PIN code that acts as a debit card password. You will enter your PIN at ATMs and debit card machines at cash registers each time you use your card.

[55]
HOW TO USE
SELF-CHECKOUT

Many places offer self-checkout machines to complete your transactions. If you are at a restaurant or coffee shop, your order and the total amount due will appear on the screen. Confirm your order is correct before paying, then insert your debit card into the slot at the bottom of the machine.

Most debit cards come with a chip on the front next to your name—insert this side into the machine. You can also tap the machine with your card at some places. Then enter your PIN code, press ENTER to confirm, and remove your card once the machine tells you to do so.

If you are at a retail or grocery store, you must scan each item yourself. First, run each item's barcode across the red-light scanner and confirm that it matches the one you're buying. Then choose PAY on the screen and pick your method of payment.

When paying with cash, insert the bills first before any coins. If you're paying with a debit card, insert the card chip side up and follow the prompts on the screen to finish your transaction.

[56]
HOW TO TIP

Tipping is the act of paying someone extra for the service they are providing. Typically, tips are between 10%-25% of the cost of the bill. Most people tip 15% for good service and 20%-25% for excellent service.

You may be prompted to tip by the machine when you pay with a debit card. You might also notice a line for you to add a tip on your receipt. Sometimes there are jars on the counter where customers can drop bills and change as a tip.

To determine the tip amount on any bill, move the decimal point one place to the left and multiply that amount by two.

For example:

The total of your bill was $12.00.

Find 10% by moving the decimal point one place left, giving you $1.20.

Multiply $1.20 by two gives you $2.40

$2.40 is a 20% tip on a $12 bill, a fair tip for good service.

[57]

PREPARING FOR
YOUR DRIVING TEST

Getting your driver's permit and learning to drive is one of the biggest milestones you will achieve as a teenager. Learning to drive comes with a lot of responsibility, not just for yourself but for every other driver on the road.

Before taking a driver's test, you may be able to take a driver's education course at school. This can give you the practice you need to feel confident behind the wheel.

If you can't sign up for a driver's ed class, you can practice braking, backing up, parking, and turning in an empty parking lot. You can also find quiet neighborhoods and cul-de-sacs to practice maintaining a speed limit and looking out for pedestrians. Be sure that you have a qualified adult with you at all times when operating a moving vehicle.

The best way to prep for your driving test is to follow this checklist:

__ Adjust seats, side mirrors, and rearview mirror before starting the car.

__ Fasten your seatbelt before putting the vehicle in drive.

__ Use turn signals and check mirrors and blind spots before turning or changing lanes.

__ Keep both hands on the steering wheel at all times.

__ Always stay within 5mph of the posted speed limit.

__ Come to a complete stop and count to three at every stop sign.

__ Maintain at least a car-length distance between you and the vehicle in front of you.

[58]

PUMPING GAS AND CHARGING ELECTRIC CARS

When you learn to drive, one of the first things you'll do is pump gas or charge your electric vehicle (EV). To charge an EV, remove the charging station connector from its dock and insert it into the car's charging port. You can open the charging port via the car's touchscreen or by gently pressing on the port door.

To pump gas, pull into an available pump and turn off your car. The arrow on the fuel gauge in the dashboard should tell you which side the gas tank is on. A button on the floor near the driver's side seat may open it, or the tank cover may be opened manually.

You're required to pay before you pump gas. You can either pay at the pump with your debit card or go inside. Then, choose the type of gasoline you want. Most vehicles take regular, but you'll want to use mid-grade or premium fuel if you drive a high-performance vehicle. A separate nozzle usually designates diesel fuel.

Unscrew the cap to the gas tank, insert the nozzle securely into the tank, and begin fueling by holding the trigger down on the nozzle. You don't have to worry about overfilling your car — the pump will automatically stop when the gas tank is full.

When you're finished, put the nozzle back. Screw the gas tank cap back on until it clicks once, and close it.

[59]
READING A MAP

You'll never be lost if you know how to read a map. It's an excellent skill for outdoor hobbies like hiking or camping.

Pick up an atlas or roadmap from a bookstore, library, or gas station and start exploring. Check the map's orientation to verify north, south, east, and west, and refer to the legend for any campgrounds, highways, or other landmarks you can use to find where you are on the map.

Use a ruler to measure the distance between you and your destination. The scale on the map will give you a ratio that you can use to determine how far away you are and how long it will take you to get there.

Once you know how far you have to go, look for a road or hiking trail nearest you on the map and follow it to your destination. There may be multiple ways to get there, so remember that the fastest route between two points is usually a straight line.

If you get lost, start over again wherever you are. Look for landmarks and pinpoint your new location on the map. Then, find the nearest route that leads toward your destination.

[60]
TAKING THE BUS

Most cities require riders to buy a bus pass. The average bus pass costs between $1.00 and$3.00 per day.

- **Buy your bus pass when you board the bus.** Insert cash into the machine by the driver, which will print out your daily, weekly, or monthly bus pass.
- **Buy your bus pass on a mobile app.** If your city provides a transportation app, you can download it and use it to buy bus passes online, and the driver will scan your pass when boarding.
- **Buy your bus pass online.** Visit your city's transportation website to pay for, download, and print bus passes.

Every bus is numbered and follows a specific route that corresponds with that number. Bus stops designate which buses stop there with the same numbers, and you can use the bus route map to find the stop closest to you.

Visit your city transportation website and click the link for bus routes. Then, follow these steps to find your bus and map your route:

- First, locate your street (or closest street) on the bus route map.
- Then, locate the bus stop closest to your street and the bus numbers that stop there.
- Finally, find your destination on the bus route and note which bus stop is nearest and the bus number that stops there.

Bus routes are often indicated by different colors. If you need to transfer to another bus, note which bus arrives at your destination. Find a stop where the bus route from your home and the bus to your destination cross over—this is where you will make your transfer.

[61]
HOW TO CALL AN UBER/TAXI

You may find yourself in a situation where you'll be without a vehicle or other modes of transportation. In these instances, you can call a taxi or use Uber or Lyft.

You can often hail a taxi directly from the street, especially at airports or in big cities. Hold up your hand and wave out to a taxi. It will pull up in front of you, and you can get in the back seat. Tell the driver where you want to go and give the specific address.

Uber and Lyft are similar to taxis. These rideshare services connect you with nearby drivers using a mobile app. Download the app to your smartphone or tablet to get a ride:

- Create an account with your phone number, email, and debit card to log into the app.
- Type your destination where it says, "Where to? _____."
- Select the Uber size you need (Hint: UberXL is for four riders or more).
- Confirm your location and choose "Request."

Once the driver accepts your ride, follow them on the map and be ready when they arrive. Make sure the license plate number and driver match the vehicle and driver in the app. Do not get into a car you don't recognize or feel comfortable in.

[62]
WHAT TO DO
AT THE POST OFFICE

Head to your local post office to mail letters, send packages, and purchase stamps.

You can put stamped letters in the blue mailbox outside the post office, but larger packages require additional postage. Follow these steps to ship a package with the self-service machine:

1. **Measure your package.** Get the dimensions by measuring length x width x height.
2. **Weigh your package.** The cost of postage is determined by how much the box weighs.
3. **Pick your shipping method.** Standard ground shipping takes 2-8 days to arrive, or you can pay more for Priority or Express shipping.
4. **Address your package.** Include the full name, street address, city, state, and ZIP code.
5. **Pay** for the postage.
6. **Print** the shipping label.

Always confirm the address is correct before printing the label. Place the label on the front of the package, so it's easy to read, and write your return address in the top left corner.

If you go to the counter instead, the postal service clerk will measure and weigh the package and print the shipping label for you.

[63]
WHAT TO DO
AT THE PHARMACY

When you pick up or refill a prescription, bring your health insurance card and I.D. Hand these over to the pharmacist and give them your name, your doctor's name, and the name of the medicine.

The pharmacist will use this information to verify your insurance and fill the prescription. If you have questions about your medication, you can confirm with the pharmacist. However, if you don't want to ask something personal in public, you can call the counter from home and ask to speak with the pharmacist.

It's important to read the information sheet that comes with your prescription and follow the dose precisely as prescribed by your doctor. Contact your doctor directly if you experience any side effects from your medication.

[64]

WHAT TO DO
AT THE AIRPORT

It's always a good idea to arrive at the airport at least two hours before your flight. This will give you plenty of time to print your boarding passes, get through security, and find your gate.

Head to the desk associated with your airline and present them with your I.D. to check in. They will confirm your flight, check your bags, and print your boarding pass.

Sometimes the check-in line is very long. Download the airline's mobile app to check in the night before and get your boarding pass digitally. If you don't have the app, use the airline's website and print your boarding passes at home.

When you enter the security line, place all of your items on the conveyor belt where security can look at them through an x-ray camera. You may be asked to remove your shoes and remove any liquids or electronics from your bag. As security checks your items, you will walk through a metal detector or full-body scanner.

After security, confirm your flight time and gate on the large Arrivals & Departures screens:

From the left, your destination city is listed first, followed by the airline and flight number. The gate is listed to the right with an alphanumeric. Check your boarding pass to confirm that your flight is on time.

SECTION FOUR

WHAT HAPPENS AT HOME

There are many different types of homes, with rooms, appliances, furniture, and more, that can represent new opportunities or obstacles for you as you grow.

Knowing what to do with some of the tools and machines around your home can help you finish tasks faster. It will also prepare you for when you eventually move out on your own.

Most home emergencies are easily avoided when you pay attention to what you're doing and act responsibly when using major appliances, like stoves or washers and dryers. However, accidents are bound to happen, and some things are beyond your control.

For example, does your family have a plan in place in case of fire? It's important to know where all the safe exits are in your home and have more than one way out in case of an emergency.

[65]

DEALING WITH
A FIRE AT HOME

Fires can happen without warning. Most home fires occur in the kitchen, but you can prevent flames from spreading by:

- **Smothering grease fires.** Flames need oxygen to breathe, so quickly cover the stove fire with a pan or smother it with baking soda.
- **Using a fire extinguisher.** Pull out the pin on the top and hold the hose while you squeeze the handles to extinguish the flames.

If the fire spreads quickly, get out immediately. Cover your mouth and nose with your shirt and crawl beneath the smoke. If door handles or window frames are hot to the touch, do not go through them. There is fire on the other side, and you need to use your secondary route.

You may not have time to grab personal belongings in a fire — do not go back for them. Once you're out of a burning building, do not go back in until the fire department says it's safe to do so.

[66]

WHEN THE POWER GOES OUT

Power outages can happen at any time. Powerful storms, surges on city power grids, or repairs to your home's breakers could cut power for a few hours or a couple of days.

If the power goes out at your house, follow these steps:

- Unplug appliances and electronics
- Keep refrigerator doors closed
- Use flashlights instead of candles
- Check on your neighbors

Unplugging major appliances will protect them from a surge when the power comes back. However, without power to the fridge means, your food will go bad quickly. Eat fresh things first and save non-perishable items in case the power outage lasts longer than a day.

[67]
WHEN THERE'S A WATER BOIL

Water boils are warnings from your city government that the water is not safe for consumption. Sewage or rain runoff can contaminate local water supplies, and residents will be asked to boil all water before cooking and drinking.

Law requires local governments to alert people when utilities are unsafe. Yours will notify you through local news, email, or automated phone calls and text messages.

If you don't have a well or clean water supply in storage, you will have to boil your tap water. Boiling water reaches 212°F, hot enough to kill any bacteria. Let your water sit at a rolling boil for one to three minutes before using it.

Can you still bathe during a water boil? Yes, but be careful not to swallow any water. You can also continue to use the toilet and wash your hands with soap during a water boil, but don't drink from the tap until the city declares it's safe.

[68]
HOW TO GROCERY SHOP AND STOCK A PANTRY

Planning meals and prepping a pantry are essential to your daily success in the kitchen. Knowing what you want to eat will help you build a grocery list.

Organize your list by department to find what you need easily in the store. For example, list your dairy foods together — milk, yogurt, coffee creamer, etc. — so you can grab them all at once as you work your way down the aisle.

Stock your refrigerator with essential items like milk, butter, and water, and keep your pantry packed with non-perishable foodstuffs like noodles, peanut butter, and soup.

Consider your favorites, like spaghetti or peanut butter and jelly, and always keep those items stocked. It's also important to keep baking ingredients in your pantry, like flour, baking soda, sugar, and spices, so you're always prepared.

[69]
FOLLOWING A RECIPE

The recipe is your guide to cooking the perfect meal—it tells you everything you need to know. Most recipes reads in the same order:

The name of the dish is listed first. Next is the serving size (or yield) and cook time. This is how many people you can feed with your meal and how long it will take to both prepare and cook the food.

The ingredients are listed with the amount needed. Most recipes use these abbreviations:

- tsp (t): teaspoon
- Tbsp (T): tablespoon
- oz: ounce
- pt: pint
- lb: pound
- g/kg: gram/kilogram

It is important to read through the entire recipe before starting because there could be important information, such as special utensils required or a specific order for combining the ingredients. For example, the recipe might call for room temperature butter, which is something you'll have to prep in advance before it is time to prepare the recipe.

The best way to get good at cooking is to practice. However, there are a few things that are helpful to know. I've listed these tips over the next short paragraphs in no particular order.

Always mix dry ingredients and wet ingredients separately. When it comes to combining the two, always add the wet ingredients to the dry ingredients instead of the other way around. Before adding the wet ingredients, create what is known as a "well" in the dry ingredients. This is a shallow indent that creates a sort of bowl within the mix. Add the wet ingredients (even if it is just eggs) into the well.

Part of whisking is adding air into the mixture, which often affects the fluffiness of the finished product. You can use a fork if you don't have a whisk, but it is important to remember that you are not just stirring the mixture; you are whipping air bubbles into it. This is why it is important to use an up and down stirring motion at a quick speed rather than a clockwise or counterclockwise swirl.

When it comes to making crusts, the trick is to use cold butter. In fact, using almost frozen butter is a really good idea. Another thing to keep in mind is that flakey crusts are formed by creating multiple layers of butter and dough. You want to fold the dough, though, instead of kneading the dough, to get nice, flaky layers.

This brings me to my next subject, kneading. When creating bread or other pastries, it is important to pay attention to how much you knead dough. It may seem like it doesn't matter, but it really does. When you knead dough, it builds gluten, and this can make the bread too dense if it is overdone.

When it comes to combining hot and cold liquids, it is important to temper them. This means adding a small amount of the hot ingredient to the cold ingredient before combining them all together. To do this properly, put the cold ingredient into a large bowl and briskly whisk the liquid as you slowly pour a couple of ladles of the hot ingredient. The reason for doing this is to keep the cold ingredient from curdling. This is especially true for ingredients such as milk.

When making cookies (or anything really), you can tell if you added too little baking soda if they come out flat. This is because baking soda releases carbon dioxide, which helps fluff out recipes.

Salt is important in both cooking and baking. In cooking, it can help sharpen the other flavors within a dish. In baking, salt does more than just adjust the flavor — it affects yeast production. Too much salt can destroy a loaf of bread. Likewise, salt is also hygroscopic, which means it attracts water and helps prevent your baked goods from drying out in the oven.

If you add too much salt while cooking, you can always balance the flavor out by adding a tiny bit of vinegar. If your dish is too spicy, add a little bit of brown sugar or honey. If something is too sweet, you can add a little bit of lemon juice or yogurt to help.

Mise en place is a French term that is common in the kitchen. It means "everything in its place" and refers to the process of prepping the kitchen before starting your recipe. Dice, julienne, and measure everything that needs measuring before you start your recipe. Have it all prepared beforehand. You can also take this a step further by making sure your dishwasher or dish rack is empty to make clean up that much easier. As you use items, clean them or put them away to keep your kitchen from becoming an overwhelming mess while you cook.

[70]
HOW TO PLAN AND COOK A MEAL

Take a look at your pantry to see what ingredients you have. Then, gather your favorite recipes or look up new ones online to plan your next meal.

Check your schedule and give yourself at least an hour to prepare and cook your meal. If you're particularly busy during the week, you can pick one day to cook multiple meals and leave yourself leftovers. Another option is to prep ingredients in advance like browning burger or chopping vegetables.

When it comes to planning a meal, it is important to use as many ingredients you have on hand first and keep your schedule in mind. Sometimes aiming for a simple meal is a much better idea than overcomplicating things and feeling rushed. Be realistic about your energy levels as well. The last thing you want to do is go grocery shopping, spend the time planning, and then realize you are too stressed out and busy with school to cook for an hour and a half. That's a surefire recipe to end up wasting your money on takeout or fast food.

Ideally, each meal should be 50% vegetables, 25% carbs, and 25% protein. However, this is not reasonable for everyone, and it is more important to access your lifestyle and natural eating patterns when planning your meals ahead of time. You'll most likely see and hear advice regarding how much and how often to eat. It's good to strive to improve your diet, but that doesn't mean being unrealistic in your approach.

If you don't wake up with enough time to cook bacon and eggs with sauteed veggies, that's fine! A piece of fruit and a protein shake or handful of nuts is enough to get you going. If you are a snacker, only planning and shopping for large meals will end with you visiting vending machines. Plan for your natural inclinations. If you accept what kind of eater you are, it is easier to save money and plan healthier meals than if you decide to conform to someone else's idea of what food should look like.

When cooking for multiple people, it is a good idea to plan for each person to eat two servings. Larger people will eat more than this, and smaller people will eat less. If you have two adults and two children, a six-serving meal should be enough to feed everyone. However, a four-serving meal might leave someone hungry.

If you are low on money and have many people to feed, broth-based soups are always a good call. Rice and bean dishes are also a good idea. Limiting meat will help to keep costs down. Lentils and chickpeas are excellent and affordable protein substitutes for some meals. If you practice, you can make a decent loaf of bread with packets of active yeast, flour, salt, sugar, oil, and water. Learning to make bread is a simple and impressive way to feed many people with little.

Casseroles are fun recipes to try because you can easily swap ingredients. For example, use extra cream of chicken soup if you don't like mushrooms.

You can also use ground beef or tofu instead of chicken. However, different proteins cook at different temperatures, so adjust your cooking times and use a thermometer to ensure you're cooking everything at the right temperature.

[71]
HOW TO BREW COFFEE AND TEA

Practice extra care when brewing hot beverages to avoid getting burned. The safest options are auto-drip coffee makers or kettles.

To brew coffee in an auto-drip coffee maker, choose how many cups you want and add water to the fill line. Next, put your filter in the basket and add 2 tbsp of grounds for each cup you're making. Close the basket, turn it on, and wait for your coffee to brew.

For teas, you will need an electric kettle or a regular kettle to boil water on the stove. For an electric kettle, add water to the fill line, place it on the heating plate, and turn it on. Traditional kettles are filled with water and put on the stove. Turn the burner to medium-high and wait for the whistle, which means the water is boiling.

Add the tea bag to your cup and slowly pour the hot water. Fill your mug but leave room for any cream or sweetener you want to add. Let the tea steep for three to five minutes before removing the bag, then let it cool for another two to three minutes.

[72]

HOW TO LOAD
A DISHWASHER

There's no wrong or right way to load a dishwasher, but knowing how to organize one will lead to cleaner dishes!

- **Put plates on the bottom rack.** The thin slots at the bottom are designed for plates of all sizes.

- **Put mugs and cups on the top rack.** Line cups up on the outer sections of the top rack.

- **Always put plastics on the top rack.** Plastics can melt if washed on the bottom rack.

- **Load forks and spoons handle first.** Silverware isn't properly sanitized when washed handle-up.

- **Load knives and cutlery handle-up.** Blades should always point downward when you're washing dishes to avoid cuts.

- **Place cutting boards and cookie trays on the outer sections of the bottom rack.** If there is no room, wash them by hand.

When you're ready to wash, add detergent to the soap compartment on the dishwasher door. This compartment usually has a latch—open it to add the soap, then close it again before closing the dishwasher.

Lock the dishwasher before you choose your wash cycle. You can also choose between a cool or heated drying cycle.

[73]
CLEANING AS YOU GO

There are plenty of odd jobs around the house—cleaning your room, changing a lightbulb, or sewing up that hole in your jeans.

So rather than putting these chores off for later, tackle them head-on and get them out of the way.

Being handy is about being efficient. The chores you're responsible for now will stay with you as you grow, but you don't have to spend your whole day fixing things and cleaning. Learning ways to work smart is essential to finding a happy balance in your adult life.

Keeping a clean home is vital to your physical and mental health. Clean rooms and surfaces prevent sickness from spreading, and decluttering your space will help relieve stress.

An easy way to clean up quickly is to bundle tasks and clean as you go. For example, if you know you need to vacuum your bedroom, dust your shelves and other surfaces while you pick things up. This way, by the time you're done vacuuming, your room is completely clean, and you're already done.

Other ways to bundle cleaning chores together:

- Wipe down the bathroom sink while/after brushing your teeth.
- Wash the dishes while you wait for dinner to cook.
- Make your bed when you get dressed in the morning.

Another way to clean faster is with a daily, weekly, and monthly schedule of cleaning tasks. Incorporate them into your routine one at a time. Eventually, you won't even notice that you're cleaning up, but you will appreciate consistently having a clean space.

[74]

CHANGING
LIGHTBULBS

Changing a lightbulb is easy when it's done safely. The first thing you want to do is turn off the light switch. Cutting the power prevents shocks and possible electrocution.

Wait five to ten seconds for the bulb to cool before touching it. If you need to climb a ladder to change a lightbulb, ask an adult for help. Otherwise, remove the lampshade and carefully unscrew the bulb.

Every lamp is designed for a specific wattage. The lamp's wattage is typically written on a sticker around the bulb socket. The wattage of each bulb is written on the top. You'll want to use a replacement bulb that matches the wattage of the lamp.

Confirm the watts on your new bulb before screwing it into the socket. Then, turn the bulb clockwise to secure it tightly. You won't be able to turn it anymore when it's in place.

Finally, turn the light back on.

[75]
SEWING/MENDING CLOTHES

Holes, tears, and broken seams can happen to your favorite piece of clothing. Learning to sew can save you from having to throw things away.

Start by picking out a thread color that matches the torn garment. You can also pick a patch or swatch of fabric to cover it up and change the look. Then, flip the piece of clothing inside out and locate the tear. If it's wrinkled, iron it out before you start sewing.

Cut about twelve inches of thread and poke the end of it through the eye of the needle. Tie a knot at the other end of the thread. Then, start sewing from side to side over the length of the tear. Pinch the fabric together and pull the needle under and through the tear. Bring the needle back under the tear and the first threads and repeat this side-to-side movement over the entire tear.

You will need to backstitch over your sewing to strengthen the new seam. To do this, add two or three horizontal stitches over the side-to-side stitches you just finished.

[76]

SHUFFLING CARDS

Start by splitting the deck equally and holding one half in each hand. Next, bend the decks gently by holding the top with your thumb and pushing the middle with your forefinger. The decks will look concave as they face each other in your hands.

Slowly bring the decks together and riffle the cards with your thumb, letting them tumble in between each other. Don't let go or straighten the deck yet. Instead, bend the cards up and towards you while gently pushing down on the top with your thumb. This will create a cascading bridge as the cards fall on top of one another.

It will take practice to get your hands used to holding the decks this way, and the cards are bound to fly out of your hand at least once before they bend and shuffle. Walk away when you get frustrated, but try to practice for a few minutes every day. You'll find that you pick it up in a couple of weeks or less when you keep trying.

[77]
HOW TO USE TOOLS

Some jobs around the house will require a toolkit. You'll find your most commonly used tools in there:

Drills are used to insert screws more tightly and securely than a screwdriver. They can also be used to bore holes into the wall to seat what is known as an anchor to hold heavier items like curtain rods or shelves. There are many attachments, and often a drill kit will come with an instruction manual detailing what each attachment does. You can also find detailed instructional videos online for free.

Pliers are used to grip pipes and wires, and some are sharp enough to cut wire.

Screwdrivers come in two styles—flat and Philip's head—to match the different types of screws. A Philip's head screwdriver has a tip that looks like a cross, whereas a flathead screwdriver has a flat tip.

Wrenches fasten and loosen various sizes of nuts, bolts, pipes, and pipe fittings.

Hammers have a flat side for hammering nails in, while the claw is used to pull nails out.

Nails are essential to building and hanging anything and come in different sizes for different jobs. You can often buy nail kits that will have a large variety of sizes for a low cost.

Tape measures will help you find length and width in feet and centimeters/meters.

Saws will cut through wood, metal, and more, depending on which kind you use.

[78]
HOW TO HANG
A PICTURE

Get your photo or piece of art, a ruler, a pencil, a hammer, and sticky tack or nails. You'll need a few nails to hang framed pieces, but posters and unframed pictures can hang with sticky tack or push pins.

Next, choose the wall you want to hang your piece on and decide where it should go. When you've found the perfect spot, hold the picture flat on the wall and mark the top with a pencil.

Take a tiny bit of sticky tack and roll it into a ball. Stick it to the pencil line and gently press the photo into it and against the wall. If you're hanging a poster, apply sticky tack to all four corners for better support.

Hanging framed pictures with nails is a little trickier because nails hang better from a stud in the wall. You can find the stud by knocking lightly on different parts of the wall until you hear a firm, dull sound. If the sound is hollow and loud, there's no stud.

When you find the stud, hold the picture frame against the wall and mark the top with a pencil. Then, take your ruler and measure the distance between the top of the frame and the hook on the back.

Measure that same distance down on the wall and mark it with an 'x' in pencil — this is where you'll hammer in the nail. Leave a little space between the wall and the head of the nail, so the frame has room to hang.

[79]
TAKING SOMETHING APART AND PUTTING IT BACK TOGETHER

Deconstruction is the act of taking something apart. This can mean taking apart a watch, replacing the broken parts, and putting it back together. It could also mean picking apart your favorite book or movie and retelling the story in your own way.

You can also try breaking down that song you heard on the radio to hear all the different instruments. How would you change up the sound?

Start playing around with deconstruction by taking apart small items. Choose something you won't mind being without while you figure it out, like a broken watch or mechanical pencil.

[80]
HOW TO RIDE A BIKE

Once you learn how to ride a bike, you never forget. However, the first ride is pretty scary. Make it easier by practicing on a smooth surface far away from traffic, like your driveway.

Then follow these steps to learn how to ride a bike:

- **Mount your bicycle.** Plant your dominant foot on the ground. Then, lift your opposite leg over the bicycle and rest it on the pedal.
- **Sit down on the bike seat**. You may feel tempted to lean forward but keep your posture straight to maintain balance.
- **Push off slowly.** Keep your dominant foot planted to hold your balance until you are seated, then kick off slowly and lift it onto the other pedal.

Don't start pedaling right away until you're comfortable with the balance of the bike. If the bike starts to lean, take a foot off the pedal to catch yourself and try again. You can also close your fist on the handle brakes to stop the bike.

[81]

HOW TO CHANGE
A BIKE TIRE

You'll run into plenty of flat tires when you ride a bike. The good news is that you can change a bike tire in less than twenty minutes.

Things you'll need to change a bike tire:

- New tire tube
- Air pump
- Wrench
- Flat-head screwdriver

To remove the tire, rest the bike on its handlebars or lay it down chain side up. Switch to first gear when removing the back tire (don't worry about gears for the front) and open the quick-release lever in the middle of the wheel. Turn it counter-clockwise until it comes off, and gently lift the wheel off the bike frame.

Deflate the wheel by unscrewing the cap to the air valve—you might need a small wrench if it's tight. Then carefully remove the tire by hooking your fingers or a flat-head screwdriver under the rubber edge and popping it off the wheel frame.

Once it's off, slide out the flat tube and replace it with the new one. Inflate the new tube, but leave some room to fit it into your tire. Check the tire for holes and sharp objects before pressing the tire and tube back onto the wheel frame. Finally, fill the tube with air.

[82]

HOW TO PLANT
A GARDEN

Growing a garden at home is the easiest way to get fresh herbs, fruits, and vegetables. You can also plant flowers to attract honey bees and butterflies.

First, choose a place in your yard that gets plenty of sun in the morning but sees shade during the afternoon. Then, pick out some high-quality soil and mix it with compost if possible. Lay it loosely in your garden and push it into place with a hoe or claw.

When it's time to pick out seeds, pay attention to what season you'll be planting in to get the best blooms:

- **Spring:** tomatoes, cucumbers, sunflowers
- **Summer:** hot peppers, squash, marigolds
- **Fall:** collard greens, lettuce, chrysanthemums
- **Winter:** kale, spinach, peas

Plant your seeds deep enough and with equal space in between them for room to grow. Water them regularly, usually once a day. If you live in a very hot climate, water your plants twice a day, once in the morning and again at sunset.

[83]
HOW TO COMPOST

Composting helps to reduce climate change and improve your garden. However, there are certain items you can compost and others you cannot. Below are lists of what is okay and what is not.

Compost:

- Fruits
- Vegetables
- Eggshells
- Coffee grounds
- Tea bags
- Rice
- Grains

Do NOT Compost:

- Bones
- Fish
- Meat
- Meat products
- Dairy products
- Butter
- Oil

Think about where you want to store your compost. You have the option of indoor or outdoor compost bins. Many stores offer ceramic pots you can keep outside or in your kitchen, but you can also add compost to the community garden.

Every compost needs to start with green and brown materials, so add food scraps, dead leaves, and grass clippings to the base of your compost pile. Add your home compost to the bin regularly, mixing it up and checking the temperature. Compost piles should be warm, and you can water the pile every couple of days to keep it moist. It is a good idea to turn the soil daily as this allows oxygen into the compost.

You can also consider getting worms. Red worms are some of the best for helping your compost. They like smaller areas to live in—3x3 square enclosures are best. You can always build your own compost bin by nailing together used pallets. Often these can be picked up for free from local grocery or hardware stores. Just ask the store manager if they have any available that you can use.

[84]
HOW TO
PITCH A TENT

Sleeping in a tent can give you a feeling of freedom and fun that you don't get sleeping at home, but it also requires a little extra work:

1. Lay down a plastic tarp as the barrier between your tent and the ground.
2. Open the contents of your tent and ensure you have all the pieces, including tent poles and stakes.
3. Find the bottom of the tent and lay that side down on the tarp.
4. Build your tent poles. Some are connected with cords; others screw together.
5. Insert the poles into the corresponding flaps on the tent, usually marked by a matching number or color.
6. Raise the tent.
7. Stake the tent to the ground by securing the stakes through the tent's flaps and into the ground.

You might need to ask for help when raising the tent. Most tents will have two poles that crisscross at the top to form the tent's frame, but larger tents will have more poles and require two or three people to put up.

[85]

HOW TO START
A CAMPFIRE

If you're sleeping in a tent, odds are you're camping and need a fire to stay warm and cook dinner. Start by gathering three types of wood:

- **Tinder:** small sticks and dry leaves or pine needles
- **Kindling:** bigger sticks but still smaller than one inch around
- **Fuel:** large sticks and chunks of wood

Put a small pile of tinder in the center of the fire pit and stack kindling to build the flames. Balance the sticks like a tent if you need to cook. If you need light and warmth, stack and crisscross your kindling as if you're building a log cabin around the tinder.

Light the fire and blow gently at the base of the flames. Add more tinder as the flames grow. Once the fire is the size of your fist, start adding fuel.

Don't add too many large sticks at once, or you'll suffocate the flame. Instead, add one at a time. Continue to add sticks to maintain the fire until you're ready for bed. Put the fire out with a bucket of water or cover it with dirt.

[86]
WHAT TO DO WHEN
YOU FIND A WILD ANIMAL

You may encounter wildlife while camping or hiking, but you may also have wild animals on your property. Remember, animals are unpredictable. If they are sick or injured, do not approach them. You must contact animal control. Look up the number for local animal control and/or rehabilitation services. If you're hiking, report the animal to the nearest ranger's station.

However, there are certain situations when you can handle the animal yourself. For example, when baby animals fall out of their nest, you can help them return to safety.

Gently pick up baby birds with a towel and place them in a basket or plastic bowl. Put the basket or bowl in the nearest tree, as high as you can reach, so the mother bird can return for it.

If you find baby squirrels or rabbits, leave them where they are but put them in a shoebox with towels if it's cold. Check on them in 24 hours to see if the mother has returned. If not, contact animal control.

SECTION FIVE

WHAT HAPPENS ONLINE

Getting online is easy. However, you're responsible for all the information you post and share online.

You have to set your own boundaries when browsing the web and using social media. You need to learn where you can find trustworthy resources online and how to adjust privacy settings on your social media, email accounts, and web browsers to protect your personal information from hackers and online predators.

You may need permission from a parent or guardian to get online and create your own email and social media accounts. However, once you get online, you're in control of the kind of content you publish and put out there.

Your digital life won't be that much different from your real life, especially if you follow the social media accounts of people you know. The content you share will directly affect how people think about you, so pay attention to what you post on your timeline.

[87]
SETTING UP A SECURE WIRELESS NETWORK (WI-FI)

A wireless network turns your home into a hotspot where multiple devices can get online at once, but you need a modem and router to set it up.

Your internet service provider (ISP) will provide a modem. The modem plugs into a cable or fiber optic outlet in the wall to connect to the internet. Plug your router into the modem with an ethernet cable to transmit the signal. The ethernet cable will plug into the "WAN" port on both the router and modem.

Here's how to set up your secure network and get online:

1. Plug another ethernet cable into the router and connect it to your computer.
2. Type the router's IP address into your web browser. The IP address is found on the router or in the user manual.
3. On the admin page, type in the default username and password provided in the user manual.
4. Choose "Wireless Network" or "Wireless Settings."
5. Name your network (SSID). Use a generic name that doesn't give away any personal information.
6. Choose "WPA2-PSK" to make a password and secure your network.
7. Save changes.

It may take a moment for the router and the modem to finalize the network, but look for your network name when you search for wireless networks with your devices.

[88]
CREATING AN
E-MAIL ACCOUNT

Creating an email address will allow you to download music and mobile apps, create social media accounts, correspond with others, and play games online.

Fortunately, most websites host email for free. Check with your parents or a trusted adult to determine which website you want to use, then visit that site to create your account.

Choose the "Sign Up" or "Create an Account" options on the webpage. On the next screen, you'll be prompted to enter your name and the email address you want. Try a combination of your name, numbers, favorite band or movie, song lyrics, or a funny inside joke with your friends. Then, create a password.

Passwords are critical. Hackers can use them to get into your account, so make sure yours is complicated and hard to figure out. Most websites require passwords to be a combination of letters, numbers, and symbols to deter identity theft. So as long as you will remember it, the more random, the better!

Finally, check the box to agree to the host website's Terms of Service and click "Create Account."

[89]
HOW TO WRITE
AND E-MAIL

Who will you send your first online message to?

Before you start typing, always remember your audience or who you're writing to. Your best friend won't expect a formal email, but what about your history teacher or neighbor? Think about how you talk to these people in real life and start with an appropriate greeting.

Who would you send these email greetings to?

- "Hi, guys!"
- "Good afternoon, _____"
- Dear, _____"
- [Name],

Think about the purpose of your message. If this is a professional email about schoolwork or appointments, open with what you need right away. This way, your reader knows exactly what you're talking about and can respond as quickly as possible. Remember to use proper spelling and punctuation, so your message is easy to read.

Choosing the right font will ensure your email is easy to read. Email font sizes are usually between 10-12, and the most common types of email fonts are:

- Arial
- Cambria
- Courier New
- Calibri
- Times New Roman
- Trebuchet

You might recognize these fonts as required by your school when writing papers and other assignments because they are so easy to read.

[90]
CREATING A SOCIAL MEDIA ACCOUNT

Now that you have an active email account, you can use it to create social media accounts.

Most sites require users to be at least thirteen years old and will ask for your birthday to confirm you're old enough to use the site. If you aren't a teenager yet, get permission from a parent or guardian to create an account.

Choose "Create a New Account" or "Sign Up with _____" and pick the email option you want to use. The next screen will ask you to create a username and password, then prompt you to enter your email address.

The social media site will email you a confirmation code that you must click on or enter before you're able to use your new account. This step is necessary to verify your identity and link your email to the account. If you lose your password or can't get into your social media, the website will use this email address to get you back online.

[91]
HOW TO
USE ZOOM

Zoom is an online video-calling service that can host multiple users at a single meeting. You might already use it at school when working with friends on a group project or if you have classes online.

Hosts will invite you to a Zoom call with an email or a direct message that contains a link. Clicking on the link will take you directly to the meeting. You can also use the Zoom app or website. You don't need an account to join Zoom calls, but you will if you want to create meetings of your own.

Once you're in the meeting, you can control your microphone, camera, and the content you share with people on the call.

"Stop Video" will turn your camera off without ending the call. No one will be able to see you, but you can still see whoever is presenting. Similarly, muting your mic will not silence anyone else on the call except for you.

When you're ready to leave the call, click the red button that says "Leave." The meeting will not end automatically until every user leaves.

[92]

DOWNLOADING AND ORGANIZING FILES

Downloading content to your phone or computer allows you to save, edit, and resend different file types. For example, you can download photos of polar bears off the internet and upload them into your presentation for biology class.

1. Start by finding a picture you would like to use, then right-click on it with your mouse.
2. Choose "Save File As" from the pull-down menu.
3. Add a name for the photo so it will be easy to find later, then choose "Save."

Phones save pictures in "My Photos" apps, while tablets and computers save them to a folder called "My Downloads" or "My Pictures." Open the app or folder to access your pictures.

Follow these steps to send these photos through different applications:

- **Email:** Choose "New Message" and send your photos as an attachment. Click the paperclip image to attach a file, then choose the picture you want to send.
- **Zoom:** Click "Share Content or Camera" on the call screen, choose the folder where your photo is saved, and click the image to send.
- **Phone:** Open the photos app and choose the image you want to send. Then, click the arrow at the bottom or top left to share the image.

[93]
CONDUCTING RESEARCH

The internet is an excellent resource for learning how to do absolutely anything. It can help you study for a math test, learn another language, and more. But unfortunately, not every online resource is trustworthy.

Some people post false stories and incorrect information. It's up to you to learn how to recognize reliable sources and confirm the information you have is legitimate when you research online. As a rule of thumb, any website ending in ".gov," ".edu," or ".org" is likely to be a trustworthy source of information.

Other common trustworthy resources you can find online are:

- Newspapers
- Magazines
- Library websites
- University websites
- Local, state, and federal government websites

Libraries and universities will also have research databases students can use. You can log into many of these databases with your school email address. Talk with your teacher or school librarian about how to get into your school's research database.

[94]
HOW TO USE YOUTUBE

YouTube is a video-sharing website where users watch and react to all kinds of videos, from original short films to video game streams and movie trailers. You can also use YouTube to learn new things, like how to do a kickflip on your skateboard or what happens when you add vinegar to baking soda.

Search for videos at the top of the page, and the autofill will list the most commonly searched terms based on what you're looking for. The results page shows the videos most related to your search. You can see each video's length and read a summary before you watch.

Not sure what you want to watch? Take advantage of the menu on the left side of your page. You should find these features in the left-hand column:

Explore: Takes you to the top trending/most popular videos

Shorts: Takes you to short videos and TikToks

Subscription: Lists videos from the channels and users you follow

Library: Shows your saved videos

History: Lists your previously watched videos

Watch Later: Lists videos you saved to watch later

Liked Videos: Lists every video you ever liked

Subscriptions: Lists users and channels you follow

Browse Channels: Explore new channels and videos you've never seen before

Unlike other social media websites, you don't need to create an account to watch videos on YouTube. However, you will need an account to create a channel and post your own content.

[95]

CREATE AND
UPLOAD VIDEOS

Starting a YouTube channel is a great idea if you like to make movies, music videos, or other content with your friends. You must be thirteen years old to create a channel, but you can use YouTube Kids with adult permission if you're younger.

The first step in creating a YouTube channel is to choose a name. Once you have one, create a YouTube account with your email address. The account will be active as soon as you confirm your email, and you can update your channel name and start adding photos and videos.

You can use your phone or a video camera to record videos. Editing tools on social media apps can help you cut your videos with stickers, sound, and filters. Save the video to your phone or your computer before uploading.

When you're ready to upload your video, log in to your YouTube account and click the small video icon on the top right. Choose "Upload Video" and select the video file from the folder or app where it's saved. You can choose to post your video right away or schedule it for later.

[96]
HOW TO CODE
(HTML)

If you want to learn how to code and build your own sites or apps, HTML is a good place to start. It stands for "Hyper Text Markup Language." A Markup Language, or code, is how computers speak to one another and present information.

Every website you visit uses HTML tags and attributes to display information. HTML tags mark the start of a new element on your site, while HTML attributes add extra information to each tag. You can find cheat sheets online, which will help you remember which tags do what.

For example, the font tag is **<font size="+/-!"></font>**. The attribute (**"+/-!"**) tells this tag how large or small the font should be.

For a large font, you would type **"+16,"** while **"-5"** would attribute a smaller font. The closing tag **</font>** doesn't have an attribute because it is used to end the element. Without the backward slash (**/**), the computer won't know to stop that font size.

How do you code the sentence "Mary had a little lamb." in size 16 font?

Your line of code will look something like this: **<font size="+16">Mary had a little lamb.</font>**

There is no limit to what you can build with HTML code. However, there are many different digital coding languages out there, including C++, Python, and more. Watch coding videos on YouTube to learn more, or download free HTML editors from Google for more practice.

[97]
HOW TO THINK OF STRONG PASSWORDS

Your passwords are your first and strongest defense against hackers who want to steal your personal information. Reduce your risk of identity theft by protecting your networks and social media accounts with discreet and complicated passwords.

Want to think up an un-hackable password? Ask yourself these questions:

- **Is the password unique?** If you've used this password before, think of another one.
- **How long is your password?** Most sites require passwords to be between 8-20 characters.
- **Does the password use a mix of characters?** Use letters, numbers, and symbols to create an uncrackable password.
- **Will I remember this password**? Don't make a password so long and complicated it's impossible to remember.

Are passwords the only way to protect your accounts? No. Many websites offer multi-factor authentication that protects their users with security questions. You will choose the questions when you create the account, and the answers will be private to you.

[98]
RECOGNIZING ONLINE SCAMS

Online scams are instances when someone is pretending to be something they're not to get money or information from you. For example, you might receive an **email scam** saying you've just won, but you have to click on the link to claim your mystery prize—don't!

Never click any links from email addresses you don't recognize. If you receive such an email, delete it immediately.

Another very common online scam is **phishing**. Phishers may use your friends' social media accounts to send messages. They might say you're locked out of your account and threaten you until you give away the password—don't!

Your passwords protect your identity, and phishers will use that information to steal and create false accounts.

Have you experienced other kinds of online scams? What about scams disguised as antivirus software? This will look like a pop-up window that says your device is infected with a virus. It will ask you to install software to resolve the issue—don't!

This is a **malware scam**. The software will hack into your network and steal personal information from any device connected to it.

[99]

RECOGNIZING SHOPPING SCAMS

Online scams can appear on shopping websites. Scammers will create fake web pages that look just like the original to trick shoppers into entering credit card numbers, home addresses, and other identifying information.

When shopping online, stick with websites you trust and have shopped with before. Verify the URL to confirm you're on a legitimate site. For example, http://www.amazon.com is the URL for the online retailer Amazon.

Never click on links to open new windows or tabs that take you away from your shopping site. This is known as **formjacking,** where hackers direct shoppers to similar-looking websites and request payment and shipping information.

Formjacking will have similar URLs that are different by only a letter or two. Look closely and see if you can spot the real URL from the scams in this list:

- http://www.ammazon.com
- http://www.amazzon.com
- http://www.amazon.net
- http://www.e-amazon.com
- http://www.amazon.com
- http://213.136.120.240/.amazzon.com

Some scam links are different by one letter, which can be easy to miss. Hackers rely on that, so always double-check you're on the right site before entering your payment information.

[100]
RECOGNIZING AND REPORTING ONLINE PREDATORS

Do you have online friends who you play video games with or talk to on social media? Do you have followers on social media who you don't know in real life? It's important to remember that these people are strangers, even if you seem to have a lot of things in common.

How do you know if you can trust someone online? Look out for these suspicious behaviors when you're chatting with them:

- Are they always asking for pictures of you or video calls?
- Are they angry when you aren't online?
- Do they ask you to keep secrets?

- Have they sent you gifts in the mail?

If you answered yes to one or more of these questions, it's best to stay away from this person online. You can block their account from following yours on social media and report the user to the forum or website moderator.

If someone is very aggressive with you online and continues to harass you for photos or other inappropriate behavior, call the police or 1-800-843-5678 to report a predator.

[101]
WHAT HAPPENS WHEN YOU SHARE PHOTOS ONLINE

It's very important to be aware of the photos you share with people online. People should never ask for pictures of you or your friends, but the things you share on social media websites like Facebook, Instagram, and Twitter are available to the public.

Once you post a picture online, there is no way to know who will see it, share it, download it, or make a copy. There is also no way to delete a photo from the internet once you post it. Yes, you can delete posts from websites and social media, but it's impossible to trace every copy made.

You can protect your photos by making all of your social media accounts private. This means that only people who follow you can see your posts. It will also protect your photos from coming up on different search engines.

However, if you tag friends in photos, those pictures will be seen by more than just your friend list. Therefore, you should only tag people you trust. You can also ask your friends not to tag you in photos to further protect your identity online.